U.S. HISTORY IN REVIEW

The Dust Bowl

Emmett Martin

Enslow Publishing

Please visit our website, www.enslow.com. For a free color catalog of all our high-quality books, call toll free 1-800-398-2504 or fax 1-877-980-4454.

Portions of this work were originally authored by Marie Roesser and published as *The Dust Bowl*. All new material this edition authored by Emmett Martin.

Cataloging-in-Publication Data
Names: Martin, Emmett.
Title: The Dust Bowl / Emmett Martin.
Description: Buffalo, NY : Enslow Publishing, 2027. | Series: U.S. History in review | Includes glossary.
Identifiers: ISBN 9781978547070 (pbk.) | ISBN 9781978547087 (library bound) | ISBN 9781978547094 (ebook)
Subjects: LCSH: Dust Bowl Era, 1931-1939–Juvenile literature. | Dust storms–Great Plains–History–20th century–Juvenile literature. | Great Plains–History–20th century–Juvenile literature. | Depressions–1929–United States–Juvenile literature.
Classification: LCC F595.M327 2027 | DDC 973.917–dc23

Published in 2027 by
Enslow Publishing
2544 Clinton Street
Buffalo, NY 14224

Designer: Leslie Taylor
Interior Layout: Tanya Dellaccio Keeney
Editor: Therese Shea

Photo credits: Series art (grunge flag) Andrey Kuzmin/Shutterstock.com; series art (stamp icon) Stocker_team/Shutterstock.com; series art (font) santstock/Shutterstock.com; series art (swash) BUTENKOV ALEKSEI/Shutterstock.com; cover (main), pp. 5 (top), 13 Everett Collection/Shutterstock.com; p. 5 (bottom) Foxys Graphic/Shutterstock.com; pp. 7, 21 (top), 25, 29 Courtesy of the Library of Congress; p. 8 https://upload.wikimedia.org/wikipedia/commons/6/67/Bank_of_the_United_States_failure_NYWTS.jpg; p. 9 https://upload.wikimedia.org/wikipedia/commons/6/61/Poor_mother_and_children%2C_Oklahoma%2C_1936_by_Dorothea_Lange.jpg; p. 11 https://upload.wikimedia.org/wikipedia/commons/b/bb/Farmer_walking_in_dust_storm_Cimarron_County_Oklahoma2.jpg; p. 15 https://upload.wikimedia.org/wikipedia/commons/1/1c/Dust_storm_in_Spearman%2CTexas%2C_Wea01422.jpg; p. 17 https://upload.wikimedia.org/wikipedia/commons/d/d2/Dust_storm_approaching_Stratford%2C_Texas.jpg; p. 19 (top) https://upload.wikimedia.org/wikipedia/commons/5/54/Lange-MigrantMother02.jpg; p. 19 (bottom) https://upload.wikimedia.org/wikipedia/commons/3/3e/Dust_Bowl_farmers_of_west_Texas_in_town.jpg; p. 21 (bottom) https://upload.wikimedia.org/wikipedia/commons/5/55/Young_Oklahoma_mother%2C_age_18%2C_penniless%2C_stranded_in_Imperial_Valley%2C_Callifornia_-_NARA_-_195849.tif; p. 23 https://upload.wikimedia.org/wikipedia/commons/7/72/Plains_farms_need_trees_LCCN98517930.jpg; p. 27 (Guthrie) https://upload.wikimedia.org/wikipedia/commons/0/09/Woody_Guthrie_2.jpg; p. 27 (Lange) https://upload.wikimedia.org/wikipedia/commons/c/cd/Dorothea_Lange_atop_automobile_in_California_%28restored%29_%28cropped%29.jpg; p. 27 (Steinbeck) https://upload.wikimedia.org/wikipedia/commons/d/d7/John_Steinbeck_1939_%28cropped%29.jpg.

Printed in the United States of America

CPSIA compliance information: Batch #CSENS27: For further information, contact Enslow Publishing, New York, New York, at 1-800-398-2504.

Contents

Words in the glossary appear in **bold** *the first time they are used in the text.*

The Deadly Dust Bowl

In the 1930s, a large part of the **Great Plains** was hit with long **droughts** and powerful dust storms. This area and these events were called the Dust Bowl. Thousands died, and more than two million had to leave the Great Plains. Read on to find out how the Dust Bowl happened.

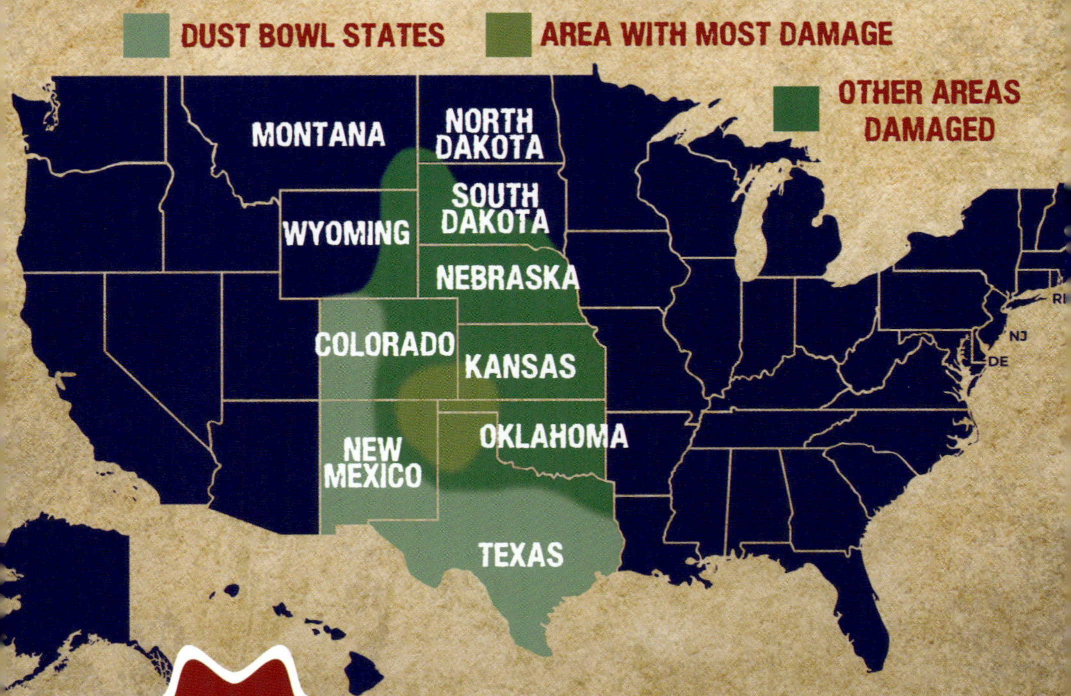

Learn More

The Dust Bowl affected parts of Colorado, Kansas, Texas, Oklahoma, and New Mexico hardest.

Changing the Land

In the mid-1800s and early 1900s, the U.S. government allowed settlers to claim land on the Great Plains. Some used the grasslands to raise livestock. Others cleared land to farm crops. In the early 1900s, wheat was in high **demand**. More farmers began to clear even more land to grow wheat.

Learn More

World War I was fought from 1914 to 1918. It was one reason for the demand for more wheat. Soldiers needed bread to eat.

In 1929, the Great Depression began. During this tough time, banks failed, and people lost jobs, savings, and homes. The prices for wheat and other crops fell. So, farmers on the Great Plains planted more crops on more land to try to earn money.

protest at failed bank

Learn More

The Great Depression didn't end until after the United States entered World War II in 1941. The war created many new jobs.

family during the Great Depression

A Time of Drought

The 1930s brought drought years to the Great Plains. Without enough rain, farmland dried up and crops died. Much of the natural grasslands had been cleared for farming and **grazing**. The land lacked plant roots to keep soil in place during strong winds.

Learn More

Plant roots also hold **moisture** in the soil.

Whipping Winds

When high winds blew through the flat Great Plains, they easily picked up the dry soil. Windstorms became dust storms. Sometimes the storms lasted for days. Some powerful winds carried so much dirt that they blocked sunlight.

Learn More

Some dust storms carried dirt as far as the East Coast of the United States.

Dust Storm Dangers

Dust storms were dangerous. Winds filled with dust and stones hurt people. Dust got into people's homes, food, and water. Sometimes roofs of homes fell in because of the added weight of the dust. People became sick from breathing in the dust. Many died.

Learn More

About 7,000 people died from what was called "dust pneumonia," from breathing in dust in the air.

Black Sunday

April 14, 1935, became known as Black Sunday. On that day, a dust storm hit Oklahoma and then moved south into Texas. The storm created a moving wall of dust that looked like a **tsunami**. It's thought that the storm moved about 60 million pounds (27 million kg) of soil.

Learn More

A news reporter writing about Black Sunday said it had started in the "dust bowl." This was the first time these words were used.

Forced to Move

The Dust Bowl wasn't just a day or a month. It took place over years. The long-lasting terrible conditions forced more than 2.5 million people in the Great Plains to move. They needed food and money. However, with the Great Depression going on, there weren't many jobs.

Learn More

Dorothea Lange took many photographs of people during the Dust Bowl and the Great Depression, like the ones shown here.

People leaving the Dust Bowl were not welcome in some places. Some people worried these **migrants** brought illness and crime with them. Sometimes police even stopped the migrants from entering cities and towns. Many migrants had to live in tents or poorly built houses called shanties.

Learn More

Some called the Dust Bowl migrants "Okies," even though they didn't all come from Oklahoma.

SCOTCH
SOAP

Making Changes

In 1935, the U.S. government began a project to fight the effects of the dust storms. Millions of trees were planted across the Great Plains to help break the force of the winds and retain moisture in the soil.

Learn More

The Soil **Conservation** Service began to teach new farming methods to fight the problem of soil **erosion**. The government also gave farmers money to set aside land as grasslands and forests.

A Slow Recovery

After the United States entered World War II, there were more jobs in U.S. cities for Dust Bowl migrants. They helped prepare the nation for war. Some became soldiers. Rainfall returned to the Great Plains by the end of 1939. Farms **recovered**.

Learn More

The government bought land from farmers and ranchers and replanted grasses. National grasslands still exist today on the Great Plains.

Dust Bowl Memories

The Dust Bowl deeply affected Americans. This is reflected in **culture**. Musicians such as Woody Guthrie wrote songs about it. Writer John Steinbeck wrote about it in his famous book *The Grapes of Wrath*. The work of photographers such as Dorothea Lange showed people's suffering so that they wouldn't be forgotten.

Learn More

Woody Guthrie traveled with Dust Bowl migrants to California and learned songs that they sang.

Woody Guthrie

Dorothea Lange

John Steinbeck

After the Dust Bowl

Crops and other plants began to grow well again on the Great Plains in the 1940s. The Dust Bowl taught farmers and the government about the **consequences** of not preparing for droughts and storms. They learned about conservation too. The lessons of the Dust Bowl should not be forgotten.

Learn More

In the 1950s, a two-year drought and windstorms hit the Great Plains. However, the harm wasn't as bad as during the Dust Bowl because of the grasslands and better farming practices.

A Timeline of the Dust Bowl

1929
The Great Depression begins.

1930
The first of many droughts begins on the Great Plains.

1931
Dust storms begin.

1932
Fourteen dust storms are reported.

1933
Thirty-eight dust storms are reported. The U.S. government begins to teach Plains farmers about ways to stop soil erosion.

1935
The Black Sunday dust storm hits the Dust Bowl. The Shelterbelt Project of the U.S. government begins to plant trees in the Great Plains.

1939
Regular rainfall patterns return to the Great Plains, but millions of Americans have left the area.

Glossary

consequence: The result of an action or event.

conservation: The care of the natural world.

culture: The beliefs and ways of life of a group of people.

demand: A powerful need for something.

drought: A long period of very dry weather.

erosion: The act of wearing away by water, wind, or ice.

graze: To eat grass in a field.

Great Plains: An area of flat, open grassland in central North America.

migrant: A person who goes from one place to another often to find work.

moisture: Water.

recover: To return to a normal state after a hard time.

retain: To keep something.

tsunami: A huge wave of water created by an underwater earthquake or volcano.

For More Information

Books

Becker, Trudy. *The Dust Bowl*. Mendota Heights, MN: Apex Editions, 2024.

Tarshis, Lauren. *I Survived the Dust Bowl, 1935*. New York, NY: Scholastic, 2025.

Website

The Dust Bowl
www.ducksters.com https://www.ducksters.com/history/us_1900s/dust_bowl.php
Read more about why the Dust Bowl is considered one of the worst U.S. natural disasters.

Index